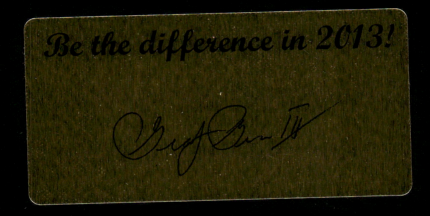

Be the difference in 2013!

JOHN MURPHY

THE HOW OF...
WOW!

♔

Secrets Behind WORLD CLASS SERVICE

Copyright© 2012 Simple Truths, LLC

Published by Simple Truths, LLC
1952 McDowell Road Suite 300
Naperville, Illinois 60563

Design: Lynn Harker, Simple Truths, Illinois
Edited by: Simple Truths Editing Department

Simple Truths is a registered trademark.
Printed and bound in the United States of America

ISBN 978-1-60810-155-9

800-900-3427
www.simpletruths.com

04 WOZ 13

"If we **all** did the things we are **capable of doing,** we would literally astound ourselves."

— THOMAS EDISON —

TABLE OF CONTENTS

Introduction:

The How of Wow!

The Secrets:

Conclusion:

INTRODUCTION

THE HOW OF WOW!

This is a book about creating raving fans, customer advocates who go out of their way to spread the good word about the experiences they have consistently had with you. Perhaps you can relate to being a customer advocate. Maybe you were "wowed" while buying groceries, resolving a problem with your bank, checking into a hotel or flying across the country. Or maybe you were not. It seems that the secrets behind world class service are often just that—secrets!

The truth is world class service organizations know and apply certain practices that most companies do not. This is what *differentiates* them from the pack. This is what keeps them moving forward on the leading edge of innovation and change, forcing others to catch up. They do things that *exceed* customer expectations. They solve problems before customers even know there is a problem. They fill latent needs before customers know they have a need. They offer value propositions that seem impossible, yet they deliver on their word. They understand that the customer is *not* always right, **that the customer often does not know what they want until they see it.** As Lee Iacocca put it many years ago, no one ever came to Chrysler and asked for a minivan to be designed. World class organizations understand that the customer is *not* "the next one down the line" in the supply chain and that many *internal* customers have no idea what the true end-user really values. Without understanding who the *real* customers are and clearly defining value in the eyes of the end users, we have little chance of consistently getting it right. We simply offer things that require time and resources but have little positive impact on the people who ultimately pay for it.

Super positive experiences with most businesses may be rare indeed, but they are a way of life for the companies that have it right. Customer service is not a department. **It is an attitude. It is a culture. It is a collective way of seeing the world.** "Wowing" customers is not the exception. It is the rule. Exceeding expectations is not a surprise. It is planned and executed with diligence, ease and grace.

Take Disney, for example. Imagine you are standing in line waiting for a ride in one of the parks. You notice a sign that indicates you will be in line for 35 minutes. Is this a guess? Is this like listening to an airline attendant telling you the plane you are waiting for is scheduled to leave on time in ten minutes when there is no plane at the gate? Disney not only knows how long you will wait, but they pad it by a few minutes so you "think you made good time" when you get on the ride in 33 minutes. Instead of being disappointed or simply satisfied, you feel good.

If you are serious about "wowing" your customers and growing your business through genuine best practices, read on. Some of the secrets revealed in this book may surprise you. After all, if everyone knew these secrets and everyone applied them, they wouldn't be secrets.

Here is your chance to join the elite in world class service. Use these secrets to:

⊙ Identify what the customer *really* wants

⊙ Learn more about your customers' customers

- ⊙ Specify the little things that add up in a big way

- ⊙ Specify the big things that set new standards

- ⊙ Use mistakes to your advantage

- ⊙ Establish pre-programmed responses for common mishaps

- ⊙ Polish the tangibles

- ⊙ Enhance the intangibles

- ⊙ Consistently get it right

- ⊙ Feel the difference it makes to you, your customers
  and your business

As an entrepreneur and businessman, I offer these secrets to you with the best intentions. Share them with the world!

John J. Murphy

"To get what we've never had, we **must do** what we've *never done.*"

ANONYMOUS

secret one

SECRET ONE

"Service is not a list of off-the-shelf solutions. It's a constant process of discovery. To be of real service, one must be willing to constantly discover exactly what the customer wants or needs—and then provide it."

Mark Ursino, former Microsoft director

Meeting obvious customer needs is good. This is what customer *satisfaction* is all about. It is like going on a blind date with someone and telling your friends afterwards that it was "satisfactory." Not much passion and enthusiasm here. In fact, some studies show that 68 percent of "satisfied" customers will take their business somewhere else when a better offer comes along. This is not customer loyalty and it is certainly not customer advocacy.

Customer advocates are consistently "wowed," not because obvious needs are met but because we are offered solutions to problems we don't even know we have. We had no idea what the Internet, or Google, or the iPod could do for us until we experienced it. And when we experienced it, we had little to say but "Wow!" Now, with the touch of a button or the click of a mouse, we can download books, reserve seats at a show, get directions to a restaurant or book an airline seat on a specific flight.

Who ordered barcodes, RFID chips, MRI scans and wireless technology? Who decided on-line banking was a good idea? Was it the customer? Why would Amazon imagine, design, create and pioneer a Kindle – an alternative to physical books and bookstores — when selling books is what originally put the company on the map? Does this seem odd? Why potentially put yourself out of business by making one of your mainstream products obsolete? The answer may not be so secretive anymore. If we do not think on the leading edge and challenge old paradigms, our competition will eat us for lunch. Sooner or later, someone else will change the rules. **The race of innovation is on-going and endless. Customers like being "wowed."**

When Chrysler sent engineers out to grocery store parking lots to observe people (predominately mothers with children) trying to load groceries into the side of a car in tight parking spaces, they uncovered an opportunity — latent needs that their customers had but never commented on. They saw the need for sliding doors and a vehicle that was not quite so low to the ground. They conceived the original mini-van, a true blockbuster.

Amazon and others are now doing the same thing with books. Just take five minutes to examine the contents and weight of a child's school backpack. Better yet, take a look at the price of some of these textbooks, particularly in college. Why not just beam the books through thin air to a lightweight template that does a thousand other things for you as well? Why not lighten the load, reduce the costs, save some trees and reduce the carbon footprint all at the same time?

The world is awakening to a field of completely new possibilities and opportunities. World class service calls for getting there first. Pay close attention to your customers. What are they struggling with? Where is the waste and clutter in the relationship? What is distracting or getting in the way? What is frustrating or annoying your customers? Do not ask if everything is okay (and hope to hear yes). This is a first level question which tells you very little. It is like asking a child how was his or her day. Chances are, you will hear a first level answer like "Fine" or "Okay." This tells us nothing. Get out and observe your customers. Order your own products. Experience what they experience. Seek to learn what is wrong or difficult or missing. Here is where you will find some of the subtle secrets to world class service – THE LATENT NEEDS.

"The *significant* problems we face cannot be solved at the same level of *thinking* we were at when we created them."

— ALBERT EINSTEIN —

"Your **SUCCESS** in life isn't based on your ability to *simply change.* It is based on your ability to **CHANGE**

secret two

SECRET TWO

THE **BIG**

"C" CUSTOMER

"Although your customer won't love you if
you give bad service, your competitors will."

Kate Zabriskie

Two of the common corporate mantras of the 1980s were "the customer is always right" and "the customer is the next one in line" (in the supply chain). Both of these seemingly obvious statements, along with other Total Quality Management mistakes, caused many companies to struggle, and even abandon TQM.

World class service organizations saw through these blanket proclamations to a more revealing truth. **The real customer is the end-user. Period.** The real customer, the big "C" customer as many organizations now call it, is the patient in the hospital, the buyer and user of the end product, the passenger, the guest and the reader.

When businesses lose sight of the end-user and start jumping to every demand of the middle people and groups, the end-user often ends up with *less* value. The process takes longer. The product costs more. There are more opportunities for mistakes, defects and delays. There is frequent misalignment, blame and finger-pointing. Without crystal clear focus on what the end user really wants and is willing to pay for, the entire supply chain can end up cluttered and costly. Thus, a **second secret to world class service is knowing the true**

customer and aligning all participating resources and people with the value stream that leads to that customer.

In a word, this facilitates *flow* – the flow of value to the customer. If I am interested in watching a specific movie on television (one that is not already scheduled to show), what is the process I must use to get the value I want? Years ago, this process might have included getting off the couch, driving to a video rental store, browsing for the movie title I want, standing in line, paying the cashier, driving home, loading a video machine and returning to the couch. The wise organization understands that most of this process is waste, non-value-added activity. Therefore, the leading edge organizations are asking, what can we eliminate to accelerate flow? How can we "wow" our customers with better, faster, lower cost and more user-friendly service? What if the customer could download a specific movie without ever leaving the couch? What if the customer could do the same thing with the bills that must be paid, hotel reservations that have to be made, or meetings that have to be attended?

The big "C" customer is what allows us to be truly aligned as a business. It is what helps us differentiate value-added from non-value added activity. It is what links and integrates the various functional departments (silos) and groups within the business. **We all have a purpose, but what is it that unites us?** What is it that pulls us together as a team? **World class service organizations know that without delighted customers, everyone is at risk.**

It is also important to note that when big "C" customers recommend your business, products or services to family and friends, it is one of the most powerful and economical sales strategies you have. To begin with, the credibility of the big "C" is high. They are giving you praise because they truly mean it. It is authentic and genuine. This is no sales pitch being offered by a commissioned or paid sales rep. It is a free tip being offered from one delighted customer to other potential customers. **The power of "Wow" is extraordinary.** For us, it has been the secret to several successful businesses and a global clientele.

"**Things** which **matter most** must never be at the mercy of things which matter least."

— GOETHE —

"No one ever attains very eminent success by simply doing what is required;

it is the amount an

of what is

excellence

over and above the required that determines the greatness of ultimate distinction."

—CHARLES FRANCIS ADAMS—

secret three

SECRET THREE

The

"The goal as a company is to have customer service that is not just the best, but legendary."

Sam Walton

One of the "formulas" world class service organizations use to "wow" customers is this:

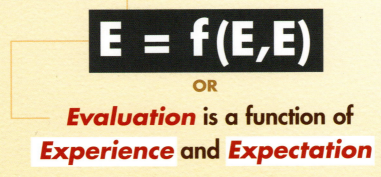

$$E = f(E,E)$$

OR

Evaluation is a function of *Experience* and *Expectation*

When we evaluate something, we compare our *actual* experience with what we *expected* to experience. If we expect to get a B in school, we are "wowed" when we get an A. When we expect to wait in line for 35 minutes, we are delighted when it takes less time. This is one of the most fundamental, yet profound secrets of "wowing" customers. To do so effectively, we must know what they expect – often based on experiences of the past and with other organizations, and what they actually experience with us. These are often referred to as "moments of truth." And wise organizations know that every interaction with a customer is a moment of truth. Every phone call, every touch point, the parking lot experience, the check-in and check-out, the packaging and of course the quality of the product and service itself are moments of truth, opportunities for "wow."

Years ago, when Lexus first entered the market, the "standard" for a vehicle recall was something like this: The customer received a postcard in the mail announcing the recall. The customer then had to schedule an appointment, bring in the vehicle, drop it off (or wait), have it repaired and check-out. This process and the repair work were touted as being free due to the mishap. No one seemed to account for the inconvenience and time involved as experienced by the big "C" customer. We all know time is money. Lexus challenged this paradigm, the status quo thinking and underlying assumptions, and changed the game. When it experienced a recall, a Lexus service representative contacted the customer and arranged to pick up the car and provide a replacement vehicle. The car was then repaired, washed and waxed, and returned with a full tank of gas and a nice gift on the front seat. Guess what a lot of people said when they experienced this level of service? No secret. The answer is, "Wow!"

Stop and consider all of the moments of truth in your business. What do your customers experience when they call you or visit your website? How difficult is it to find what the customer is looking for, order it and pay for it? How easy is it to return the product or reschedule the service if need be? How pleasant are the service reps who handle the interaction? How empowered are they to resolve customer issues and "wow" the customer with something unexpected? Do you have "pre-programmed" responses prepared for the most common mishaps?

Do your customers rave about the *positive* response they had from a negative experience? Are you turning crises into opportunities?

Imagine you take your family to a Disney park and somehow one of your children gets lost. This is a game-changing experience. One minute you are happy and excited, and then instantly you are panicked and worried. Keep in mind there are thousands of people on any given day in the Disney parks. What do you do? What might you say if you immediately went to one of the Disney information centers and they calmly informed you that your child was safe and waiting for you to return? In other words, some Disney "cast members" (as the employees are called), dressed as "guests" (as the customers are called) are always on the lookout for lost children and respond quickly with attention, care and security. **The best of the best anticipate problems**

before they surface and prepare ahead.
These are the moments people rarely forget.

"Our greatest glory is not in never failing, but in rising up every time we fail."

— RALPH WALDO EMERSON —

SECRET FOUR

"It is the service we are not obliged to give that people value most."

James C. Penney

THE
little
THINGS

Not many people can claim to be bitten by an elephant, but billions can relate to the annoyance and aggravation of a mosquito bite. Sometimes it is the little things that really weigh on people. The same is true with customer service. We will comment on the "big things" in the next chapter as they are also important to "wowing" customers, but we cannot overlook the little, everyday moments of truth. In many cases, **the little things have more impact on customer advocacy and retention than the big things.**

Forest Hills Foods in West Michigan gets this. In the very competitive world of retail and fresh food, this small grocery story shines brightly when it comes to raving customers. Why? Is it the lowest prices? No, it is not. Is it the location? No. Is it the quality of the food and products? Try again, although the quality is excellent. These are all important factors, but they are all expected. Remember, people are not "wowed" by the expected. When we go to turn on a light and hit the switch, we are not awed when the light goes on. We expect it to.

However, people are impressed when they do not have to stand in line for long periods of time, even during peak hours. We are impressed when we have our groceries delivered to our cars for us by staff who will not accept tips. We appreciate friendly attendants and warm smiles. These are standard practices at Forest Hills Foods. We are also impressed when we earn gasoline discounts for the service station in the parking lot with every purchase. The list of impressive "little things" goes on and on, and it is the culmination of these little things that brings great prosperity and promise to this thriving grocery store. **It is the combination of many small, impressive delights that add up to very powerful "wows" and loyal customers.**

In concert with moments of truth, the little things keep customers coming back. From pillows and shower heads in hotels to gourmet coffee and free wireless in automobile service centers, customers appreciate the small stuff that adds value. However, the small stuff must add value. Trivial gimmicks and meaningless schemes do not qualify as value in the eyes of the customer. **At the end of the day, the customer should feel a sense of joy and gratitude for having had the experience.** A good night's sleep in a hotel matters. A hot shower with a decent stream of water feels good. An auxiliary work center with free wireless is helpful. A friendly greeting or competent sales representative adds value. Cheap giveaways that end up in the recycle bin do not qualify as value in the eyes of the customer. **Make sure you know the difference by seeking to understand what really matters to your customers. Then act on it!**

Consider parking lots, for example. If a customer comes to your place of business for a visit, how easy is it to find a convenient place to park? Better yet, if you have thousands of people visiting in a single day, like Disney, how easy is it for guests to find their cars at the end of a long day in the park? Keep in mind this is a moment of truth that could leave an adverse lasting impression on a guest who otherwise had a positive experience. Disney understands this and once again **commits to being fanatical about detail, one of its guiding principles.** With a vice president of parking lots leading the way, Disney organizes its parking by special lot names (think Pluto or Daisy lot) and times of day. Cast members also remind guests at least three times where they parked when they shuttle them into the park. **Research shows that being reminded three times increases retention substantially.** Even so, there are people who leave the park at the end of the day and cannot remember where they left the car. How does Disney handle this? The pre-programmed response is to ask the guests what time they arrived and shuttle them to the appropriate parking lot for an easy departure. On average, this process takes about six minutes per lost vehicle with thousands of cars in the parking lots. How does Disney know?

They measure it. What gets measured gets managed. Do you hear "WOW"?

"Do what you do SO WELL that see it again

they will want to

and **BRING**

THEIR FRIENDS."

– WALT DISNEY –

SECRET FIVE

"Customer needs have an unsettling way of
not staying satisfied for very long."

Karl Albrecht

The
BIG
things

n baseball, base hits matter. In football, forward progress matters. With customer service, the little things matter. We need to move in a positive direction. We need to build momentum. **We need to execute on the little things that add up into big "Wows."** But let's admit it. Home runs and grand slams are exciting. Touchdowns and interceptions are thrilling, especially when they are game changing. Fans love to be excited and experience the unexpected in a positive way.

Game changers shift paradigms and set the competition back to zero.

New blockbuster cures for illnesses, new technologies, and new levels of service put the old standards out to pasture. Who wants to do business with a company whose products and services are obsolete? Who wants to pay money for non-value-added services and waste? Home runs can change things instantly.

World class service organizations pay attention to the little things but invest in the big things at the same time.

This wise strategy challenges the either/or mindset that bewilders many organizations and leaves them vulnerable. Amazon and Barnes and Noble are now offering new technology and products that allow customers to literally download books through thin air. Physical books are still available for the customers who want them, and the companies do an exceptional job at fulfilling orders quickly and cost-effectively. But to look only at today without an eye for the future is risky. Leading edge automotive companies are developing the next home run in fuel-efficient vehicles. Pharmaceutical and Nutraceutical companies are making giant leaps forward with alternatives to costly drugs without troubling side effects. Make no mistake, the big things matter.

Stop for a moment and think back ten years. What has changed? What kind of laptop were you using and how much did it cost? Was it wireless? Was the printer wireless? Now consider your telephone, television, car, office, kitchen, manufacturing facility or lab. How did you make things? How did you test them? How did you get directions when you were on the road? How did you buy things? How did you learn new things? What we often take for granted today was simply a concept ten years ago. Where were Facebook or Skype or Google Maps? These advancements were not small, incremental changes. They were giant leaps forward that truly "wowed" many customers. In many cases, people would find it difficult to work as efficiently and effectively today without them. They raised the bar and set new standards.

"**NEVER DOUBT** that a small group of **COMMITTED** people can **change the world.**

INDEED,

it is the only thing that ever has."

— MARGARET MEAD —

SECRET SIX

"Mistakes are the portals of discovery."

James Joyce

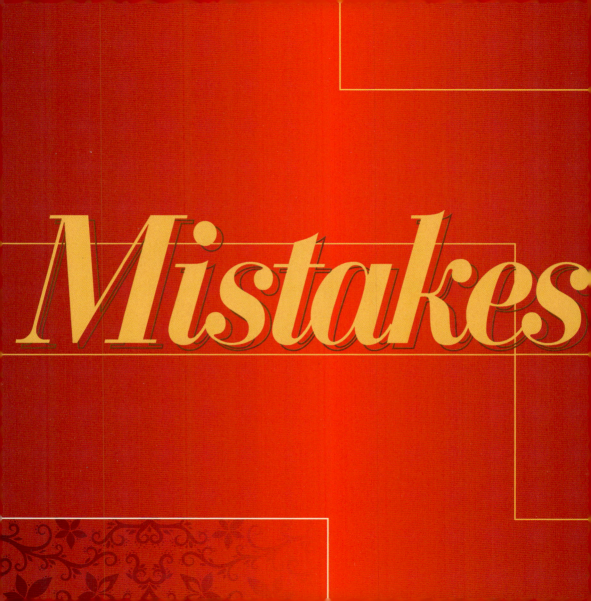

Tom Peters once said, **"We need to learn to make our mistakes faster."** In other words, **we need to learn faster.** Mistakes are often how we learn the most memorable lessons. Consider a child in early development, learning to walk and talk. Each mistake provides valuable feedback and an opportunity to learn and make adjustments. The same is true in competitive sports. There is no such thing as a game without mistakes. The key is to adjust quickly and move on.

Smart businesses use techniques like "poka yoke" (mistake-proofing) and FMEA (Failure Mode and Effects Analysis) to prevent mistakes, mitigate risk and eliminate common errors *before* they happen, but they also use methods like AAR (After Action Reviews) to evaluate what has already happened and implement corrective actions. When customers are involved, these tools are essential to turning mistakes into opportunities. The only way to get a "wow" out of a mistake is to correct it in such a way that the customer is almost glad it happened.

To do this effectively, it is wise to pull a team together and ask questions like "What could go wrong?" and "What can we do about it now?" Other good questions to ask and explore are **"What are some of our most common errors?"** and **"What exactly do we do that annoys our customers?"** Think carefully about each and every moment of truth. Annoyed customers are not raving fans. Get out and actually talk to customers. Surveys can be useful, but there is nothing as telling as honest, candid, immediate feedback on the front line. Train your team to observe customer body language, facial expressions and tone of voice. This is very telling "intelligence" that surveys do not show. **Great service organizations know how to read people and respond quickly.**

Take Mission Pointe Resort on Mackinac Island, for example. Years ago, John was visiting the resort with his family. After arriving and checking in, he and his family were waiting to claim their luggage which arrived via horse drawn buggy (while they walked from the ferry). Mackinac Island is known for its historic character and pedestrian streets. After identifying their luggage and providing the matching claim numbers, John was refused his luggage by the attendant. He insisted it belonged to someone else. At first, John found this somewhat amusing, thinking that perhaps he was on an episode of "Candid Camera" or something. It just made no sense. However, after about 20 minutes of seemingly serious debate, John asked to speak with the hotel manager. Enough was enough. The manager also refused to release the luggage, despite matching claim numbers, and even suggested that John and his family might like to stay at a different resort. At this point, the Murphy family decided to simply leave the luggage and go to their rooms. The luggage area was in complete chaos and there was no sense in making matters worse.

About thirty minutes later, John received a call from the manager apologizing for the entire situation. Apparently, there had been some kind of theft problem and the staff had overreacted. The manager then proceeded to "comp" the entire weekend, including all meals. Shortly thereafter, a beautiful bouquet of flowers arrived with a bottle of champagne and a very gracious note. John simply looked at his family and said, "Wow!"

We all make mistakes. **The secret to achieving world class customer service is not in completely eliminating or avoiding them.** In fact, customers are often more "wowed" when they have experienced a mishap and it is responded to quickly with positive impact.

The real secret is in knowing how to do this – turning a lemon into lemonade.

"Problems are *good*, not bad. Welcome them

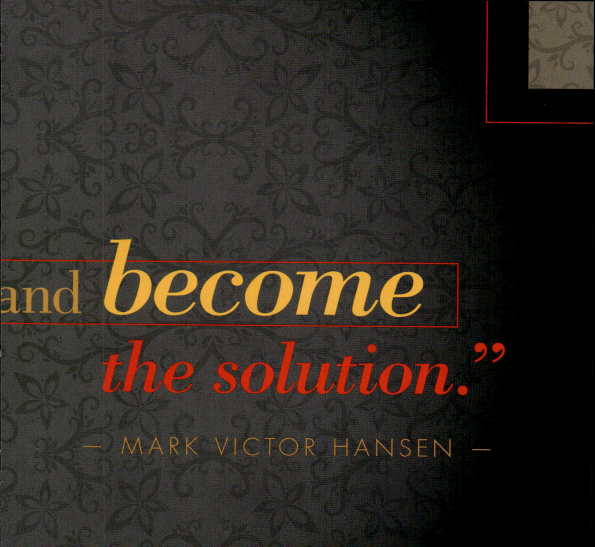

and *become* *the solution."*

— MARK VICTOR HANSEN —

SECRET SEVEN

"Sales without customer service is like stuffing money into a pocket full of holes."

David Tooman

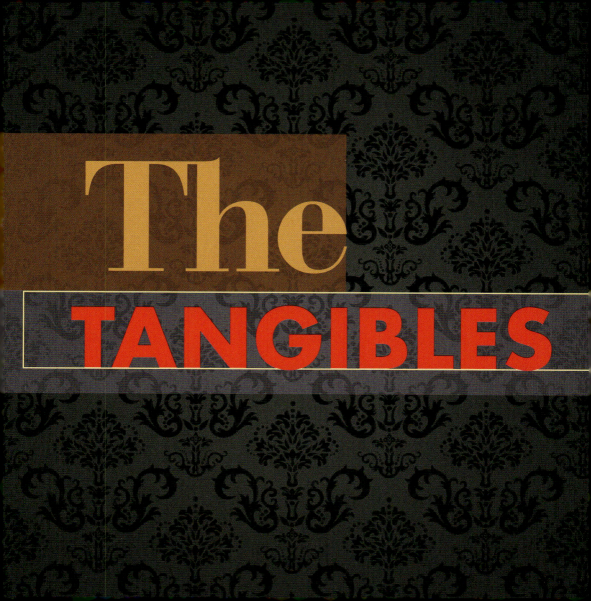

The
TANGIBLES

The tangibles are the things we see and touch. These include everything from the seats on the airplane to the website and software we used to make the reservation. When we order a product online, the tangibles include the accuracy of the fulfillment, the packaging and the efficacy of the product itself. When we walk through the store, the tangibles include the products, the shelving, the lighting, the flooring, the restrooms, the signage, the layout, the people and the checkout counter. Every tangible detail matters in some way. If the airplane seat is broken, people may worry about the rest of the plane. If the pilot looks like he is asleep, people feel uneasy. If the website keeps freezing up or is missing important data, customers get frustrated.

In a world of *total* quality and continuous improvement, customers have come to expect excellence. Anything short of *exceeding* expectations now puts us at risk. **Meeting expectations just isn't enough to cultivate genuine "wows."** Why is this? What is the secret? The answer may surprise you. ***Customers no longer compare you to your direct competition.*** Customers now compare you to every supplier and service provider they come in contact with. **The rules have changed.** If a customer has been "wowed" by someone else, they wonder why they cannot experience the same thing with you. Consciously or subconsciously, fairly or unfairly, people compare you to every other business they buy from. Stop for a moment and ask yourself, is your business Fedex fast and Disney friendly? Is your team Nordstrom aware and Amazon efficient?

Chances are your customers are in contact with some of the world's finest service organizations. They experience the websites, the showrooms, the order processes, the payment processes, the delivery processes, the packaging processes, the return processes, the human interaction, and the physical outcomes. How do you compare? How do you stand up against organizations *outside* your industry as well as inside your industry? **Are you benchmarking against the very best and bringing intuitive connections into your industry that may not exist now?**

Consider the brilliant work of Tajichi Ohno, the chief engineer at Toyota many years ago. During his benchmarking visits to the United States, he learned as much if not more from grocery stores as he did from Ford Motor Company. In fact, many of the insights and components to the Toyota Production System

(TPS) came from outside the automobile industry—changing the playing field of the automobile industry forever. For example, kanban (lean inventory pull systems) originated with the concept of milk being replenished "just in time" as need be.

What ideas are you identifying now that can be adapted and applied to your line of work that really wow your customers?

Beware of the skeptics who say "That can't work here" or "It can't be done." In this day and age, best practices are transcending industries in record time. Pay attention to what "wows" you in any given situation and ask yourself, "How can I use this practice or a variation of it in my business?" **Open your mind to the patterns and processes that many businesses share.** Exercise your intuition. Look for the connections. And remember – your customers are doing the same thing!

"The important thing is *not to* *stop questioning.* Curiosity has its own reason for existing."

ALBERT EINSTEIN

"*Quality* in a service or product put into it. *It is* or customer *get* is not what you

what the client

out of it. "

— PETER DRUCKER —

SECRET EIGHT

The

"Here is a simple but powerful rule - always give people more than what they expect to get."

Nelson Boswell

The intangibles are the things we do *not* physically see or touch. These include feelings like appreciation, love, joy, energy, emotion, intent, spirit, empathy, passion, compassion and courage. **The intangibles speak a universal language.** When a waiter or waitress is serving us a meal, how do we *feel* in the presence of this person? How do we feel in the environment of this restaurant? The tangibles certainly have impact, including the food, the beverages, the place setting, the physical environment, the sounds, the restrooms, the parking lot and the staff. In many cases, the tangibles are the easiest things to copy and compete with. Now we must consider the culture, the character, the attitudes and the spiritual energy breathing life into the establishment. Here is where the elite tend to distinguish themselves.

Customers want to feel **appreciated, loved,** and treated with **dignity** and **respect.** This is human nature at its core. We want to believe we are being taken care of in an honest, ethical and safe way. We like being called by name, attended to with a *genuine* smile, and thanked for opting to purchase from a particular vendor. We appreciate being trusted and valued. We enjoy being enjoyed. Great service organizations get this. They treat us with a feeling of honor, gratitude and grace.

Ritz-Carlton reminds its staff that it is, "Ladies and gentlemen serving ladies and gentlemen." This simple corporate mantra reflects some of the intangibles valued by this world class hotel.

Intangibles are often mood-changing. They can shift a mindset either way: from a good mood to an upsetting one or from a lousy mood to a very positive mood. What is the difference? What is it that impacts people so profoundly and sometimes so quickly? In a word it is energy. It is the "esprit de corps," the teamwork, the essence and the spirit of the people. It is Feng Shui and the *energy* of the physical environment, the layout, and the aesthetics. It is the warmth and light we feel when we enter certain environments. It is the emotional vibration we feel when we hear certain music or sounds. It is the joy we feel when we are in the presence of uplifting, charismatic energy. Stop and think about how you feel in certain environments. **What makes the difference?**

When we order a product or service over the telephone, what do we *feel* in the exchange we have with another person? What is the connection? L.L. Bean, a catalog distributor, understands that service reps have a tendency to extend what they are feeling. To enhance this "intangible" the organization trains people by putting a mirror in front of them as they speak with customers on the phone. When we see ourselves in a joyful, positive, thankful way we tend to share this feeling with others. When we smile we emit a more positive energy. The mirror simply serves as a reminder that we project ourselves onto others and at L.L. Bean the expectation is that this projection be positive and uplifting.

The same is true when we are dealing with people in person. Our physical appearances obviously vary and there are tangible things we can do to characterize the organization we represent. For example, clean uniforms and grooming requirements may have positive impact. However, many customers can relate to very negative experiences with people and organizations that get all of the "tangibles" right but fail to recognize the value and power of the intangibles.

True world class service runs much deeper than this. **The reaction of "wow" is *emotional.* To really "wow" our customers our own people must feel a sense of "wow." To accomplish this we must lead with passion and spirit in whatever role we play.** The entire team must learn to *demonstrate* wow, walking the talk and breathing life into the corporate culture. This is not someone else's job or solely the boss' responsibility. It is a choice we make personally. It is a habit we choose to form for ourselves. It helps to be in an inspiring culture—an energetic vibration – that facilitates this, but no one has to ask permission to smile and be compassionate.

What choice do you make?

"It is one of the most *beautiful comper* in life, that no man can sincerely without helping

ations

try to help another

himself."

secret nine

SECRET NINE

"We wildly underestimate the power of the tiniest personal touch."

Tom Peters

THE
empathy
and
compassion

Two of the most important "intangibles" that distinguish world class service organizations from everyone else are **empathy and compassion.** Empathy is the ability to see, hear, and feel what another human being is feeling from *that* person's point of view. Compassion is the ability to offer a person understanding, hope, and strength *without* falling to the level of despair of the one we are trying to help.

To lead someone out of grief we must see beyond grief. These leadership characteristics challenge us to transcend our own thoughts, defenses, beliefs, filters, paradigms and rationale to see as others see and act in a positive manner. Indeed, empathy and compassion are among the most important characteristics among great masters and inspiring change agents.

When a customer or potential customer contacts you, stop and consider your reaction. How do you look, feel and behave? If it is a complaint, how do you appear? If it is a question, how do you respond? If there is a problem, how well do you relate to this problem? If there is emotion involved, to what extent do you feel this emotion? Are you the solution to your customer's problem? Are you the answer to the question? Are you the resolution to the complaint? And even if the customer's needs exceed your authority, are you compassionate and under-standing or resistant and difficult? What lasting impression do you leave with this customer?

Many times, customers simply want someone to understand them and work with them toward a resolution. If the product or service is not some-thing you provide, can you recommend a reliable source that does? If the customer has been transferred on the telephone three times before reaching you, can you listen long enough to actually hear the frustration and concern and avoid a fourth transfer? If the plane to Barcelona is still at the gate while a family pleads to board it after a delayed connection, can you honestly look into opening the door—especially when the plane sits there for another 45 minutes? Your efforts may or may not result in an immediate, positive outcome, but the care and concern you provide might be remembered for a lifetime.

Genuine empathy and compassion connect people.

These critical interpersonal skills reach beyond the pretense and false identity of the ego to the authentic core of people. With focus, attention, and practice, we can lift others up from difficult situations without falling into the trap of sentimentalism or sympathy (i.e. "misery loves company"). Unlike feeling bad because someone else feels bad, empathy and compassion come from a position of wisdom and strength. We trust there is a solution. We believe we can help. We prepare ahead for common problems. Our first response is positive, not negative, and proactive, not reactive.

Several credible university studies reveal that approximately 55 percent of "impact" from communications comes from body language—how we appear when we are communicating. Another 38 percent of impact comes from our tone of voice. This leaves only 7 percent relating to the actual content of what is being said. Put simply, people are impacted more by how we look and how we sound than by what we actually say. From a customer service perspective, this is absolutely critical, especially when the contact is face to face. Obviously, it is different if we are communicating over the telephone, but a smile will still shine through.

Take time to evaluate how you look and sound when you communicate with your customers, or anyone else for that matter. To what extent do you appear **helpful, positive, joyful, competent** and **reliable**?

When you speak, do you sound optimistic? Does your appreciation for life shine through? **Do you project confidence, joy, and a positive attitude?** Do customers seek you out? Do they sense your passion and commitment to excellence?

"What YOU ARE thunders so loudly that I *cannot hear what you say* to the contrary."

— RALPH WALDO EMERSON —

secret ten

SECRET TEN

The

"Well done is better than well said."

Benjamin Franklin

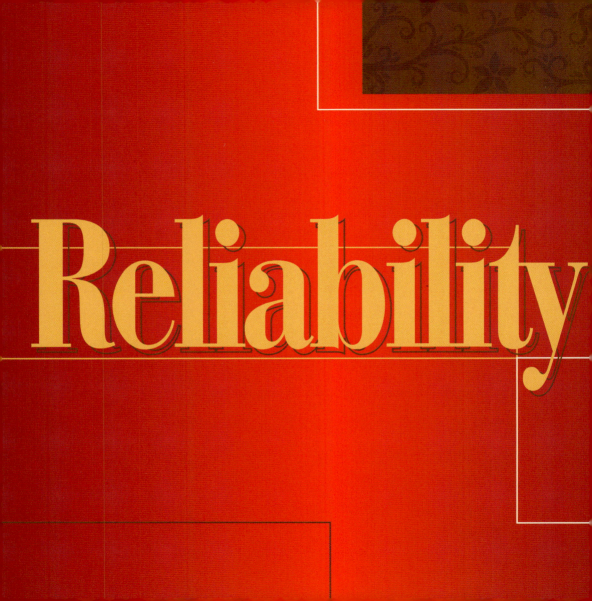

Trust is the bedrock to any healthy, lasting relationship. Like the foundation of a skyscraper, we have to have something solid to build on. We have to believe we can count on one another. We have to have faith in one another. To accomplish this we have to be honest. We have to be genuine and sincere. The help we provide to one another has to be authentic and reliable—a true win-win proposition.

Trust is particularly important in "wowing" customers. Nothing frustrates a customer more than a product that doesn't work or a service that falls short of expectation. Years of hard work and effort can crumble with one false representation or dishonest action. Customers expect more than that. We want products that last longer and perform better than yesterday's standards. We expect services that deliver results better than they did before. At the end of the day, we want to know that we are getting true value for the money we spend.

Aristotle once said that, **"We are what we repeatedly do. Excellence, therefore, is not an act, but a habit."** Once in a while quality is not enough. Periodic efficiency is not good enough. Judging by increasing world standards, we are wise to build reliability into everything we do.

We are wise to attack waste in our value streams and optimize our systems to deliver stability, predictability, consistency and security. Customers like being "wowed," not shocked.

To provide reliability, world class service organizations challenge traditional paradigms and paradoxes. For example, to be flexible we must be stable. These are not mutually exclusive, opposite poles (as some organizations think). Flexibility (for customers) without stability is simply another name for chaos. We see this over and over again in some of our consulting assignments. "Expediting" as a rule of thumb is no way to delight customers on a consistent basis. Robbing Peter to pay Paul is a poor business strategy. This would be like trying to run a safe and reliable airline without any air traffic control.

In order for Federal Express, UPS or DHL to deliver packages consistently and reliably to customers worldwide, they must maintain a stable operating system that works in harmony with their value propositions. What appears to be flexible is enabled by a very stable process. These world class service providers are not "winging it" every time they get an order. The processes and outcomes are reliable and consistent, even allowing customers to track deliveries online. Now imagine this level of service twenty years ago. Times have changed, challenging all of us to think outside the box and stretch. Our customers are doing the same.

Best practices today, like Lean Six Sigma, are being used worldwide to attack waste, reduce variation, mitigate risk, and eliminate confusion. A benchmark standard, Six Sigma performance results in approximately 3.4 defects per million opportunities. Stop and consider this. Do you know your current level of performance? How does this compare to last year? Detecting problems after they occur is useful and important, but it is also very costly — especially if these defects get out to your customers. The real secret to "wowing" customers in the long run is to shift the emphasis from detection to **prevention**. By controlling the input variables in any process, we get more predictable output variables. Think of this like baking a cake. By holding the ingredients constant, along with oven temperature and the timing, we get predictable outputs. No one has to "test" the cake to see if it is good or not. We know it is good when we know our process is stable and in control. The only way the output can vary is if the inputs vary.

Here is the real secret to *world class* **performance** and **service**:

Design and **build** RELIABILITY into your processes and let the outcomes follow. Let your reliability say, "WOW!"

"Put a *good person*
in a bad system a
WINS,

d the bad system

no contest."

—W. EDWARDS DEMING—

conclusion

CONCLUSION

10 SECRETS;

A recent new hire stepped into an elevator just as the doors were about to close. Standing there beside her was the CEO of this multi-national corporation. The CEO looked up from his smart phone, smiled, and said hello. The young recruit froze temporarily and then managed to say, "Hello, sir. How are you today?"

The CEO laughed and reached out his hand. "I am doing great. Thank you. And how are you?" His presence was powerful, yet not overbearing. He was attentive and genuine and remarkably easy to talk to. It was as if the only thing that mattered in the world to him was the exchange he was now having with this new employee. The 60-second ride seemed timeless.

Earlier that day, as a part of the new hire orientation, she had learned about the company's history, culture, mission and guiding principles. In particular, she was fascinated with the organization's commitment to excellence and customer service. It was clearly reflected in the astonishing growth this company was experiencing. She always wanted to work for a company that went the extra step to wow people. In fact, she noticed this energy throughout the day – with the receptionist, with her fellow recruits, with her boss, with her boss' boss, and with the various people she came in contact with. It felt as if it was in the air.

Within seconds of meeting the CEO she understood why. Or, at least she thought she did. "I must say, sir, that I am intrigued with the culture here. It feels very exciting. You have done a remarkable job."

Again he smiled and laughed. "Oh, thank you, but the culture is not mine. It is far bigger than me or any one person here. We work as a team. We inspire one another. I simply participate in the process and do what I can to eliminate any friction. We call this flow. It is a very creative state, quite playful in nature really. It is what allows us to imagine and innovate so effectively and efficiently. Passion is not something you intellectualize with your head. It is a heartfelt energy that connects us with one another and unites us around a shared purpose. Our purpose is clear: to wow our customers using the 10 secrets you learned about in your orientation. It is these 10 secrets that have now led us to over 10,000,000 raving customers. We think of these secrets as our seeds to success. Honor them and honor is ours. Give and we receive."

When the elevator doors opened, the CEO allowed the young recruit to exit first and then he followed. "Here is one more thing to keep in mind," he joked. **"If you ever think customers are a pain in the butt, try to do business without them."**

WE ARE WHAT WE REPEATEDLY DO.

EXCELLENCE,

then, is not an *act* but a

HABIT.

ARISTOLE

JOHN J. MURPHY

John J. Murphy is an award-winning author, speaker and management consultant. Drawing on a diverse collection of team experiences as a corporate manager, consultant and collegiate quarterback, John has appeared on over 400 radio and television stations and his work has been featured in over 50 newspapers nationwide.

As founder and president of Venture Management Consultants, John specializes in creating high performance team environments, teaching leadership and team development, and leading team kaizen events. He has trained thousands of "change agents" from over 50 countries and helped some of the world's leading organizations design and implement positive change.

John is a critically-acclaimed author and sought-after speaker. Among his other books are:

- Beyond Doubt: Four Steps to Inner Peace
- Reinvent Yourself: A Lesson in Personal Leadership
- Agent of Change: Leading a Cultural Revolution
- Pulling Together: The Power of Teamwork
- Get a Real Life: A Lesson in Personal Empowerment
- Leading with Passion: 10 Essentials for Inspiring Others
- The Eight Disciplines: An Enticing Look Into Your Personality.
- Habits Die Hard: 10 Steps to Building Successful Habits.

Please visit: www.venturemanagementconsultants.com

We purchased a Simple Truths' gift book for our conference in Lisbon, Spain. We also personalized it with a note on the first page about valuing innovation. I've never had such positive feedback on any gift we've given. People just keep talking about how much they valued the book and how perfectly it tied back to our conference message.
— **Michael R. Marcey,** Efficient Capital Management, LLC.

The small inspirational books by Simple Truths are amazing magic! They spark my spirit and energize my soul.
— **Jeff Hughes,** United Airlines

Mr. Anderson, ever since a friend of mine sent me the 212° movie online, I have become a raving fan of Simple Truths. I love and appreciate the positive messages your products convey and I have found many ways to use them. Thank you for your vision.
— **Patrick Shaughnessy,** AVI Communications, Inc.